MARLBOROUGH
in Colour

David Uttley

ALAN SUTTON
1984

Alan Sutton Publishing Limited
17a Brunswick Road
Gloucester GL1 1HG

First published 1984

British Library Cataloguing in Publication Data

Uttley, David
  Marlborough in colour.
  1. Photography, Architectural   2. Marlborough
  (Wiltshire)—Description and travel—Pictorial
  works
  I. Title
  779'.99423'170924   TR659

  ISBN 0 86299 033 5

Typesetting and origination by
Alan Sutton Publishing Limited
Photoset Bembo 11/13
Printed in Great Britain
by Nimsfeilde Press Limited

MARLBOROUGH
in Colour

Marlborough High Street from the air with the College buildings in the foreground

Preface

David Uttley was born in Halifax and educated at Trowbridge Grammar School. After teaching in North London he left to join the Woodrow Wyatt group of newspapers which introduced colour photographs into local newspapers. He was chief photographer with this group for a number of years. Married with four daughters he now teaches science at Pewsey Vale School and runs a thriving photographic business in his spare time.

David Uttley is, therefore, more than qualified to present this beautiful collection of colour photographs of his home town. Every aspect of Marlborough is covered from the Grand Avenue of Savernake Forest to the quiet backwater of Neates Yard. In between are aerial shots of the Town, the Green beneath its avenue of limes, the alleys, High Street, the Kennet, schools and churches and the College to build a representative picture of this delightful Wiltshire town.

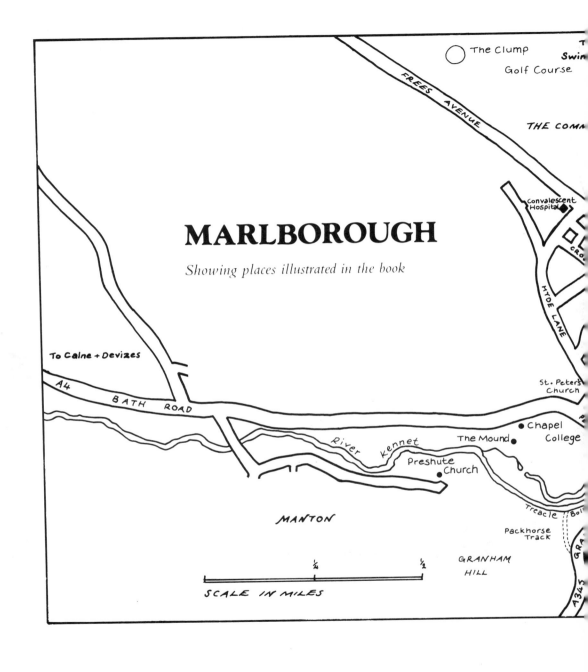

MARLBOROUGH

Showing places illustrated in the book

The Clump

Golf Course

FREES AVENUE

THE COMM

Swin

Convalescent Hospital

CRO

HYDE LANE

To Calne + Devizes

A4

BATH ROAD

St. Peter's Church

River Kennet

The Mound

Chapel College

Preshute Church

Treacle Bol

MANTON

Packhorse Track

GRA

GRANHAM HILL

A345

¼ ½

SCALE IN MILES

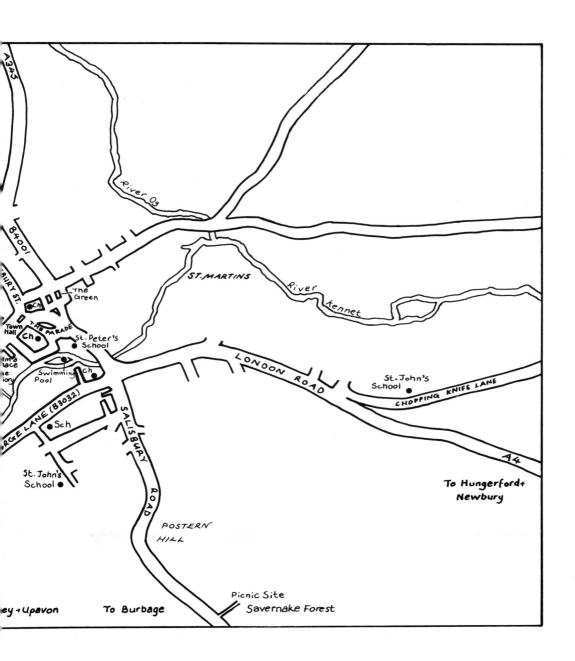

Savernake Forest

One of the main factors influencing the growth of Marlborough was the Bath Road which originally carried stage coaches from London to the West. Another important factor was Savernake Forest, a favourite hunting ground of Kings and at that time covering an area at least fifteen times larger than at present. Nearby Marlborough provided an ideal base for these Royal sporting activities.

The Forest today occupies about 4,400 acres and, whilst no longer a hunting ground, still fulfills one of its original uses – namely recreation. The Postern Hill picnic site, well organised by the Forestry Commission, now provides open spaces, camping facilities and barbecue hearths which are well used by a rather wider cross section of the community than in the past.

Savernake is bisected by its famous four mile long Grand Avenue lined by tall, graceful beech trees which have observed the passing of many forms of transport. Sadly in recent years a number of these have been felled as they became dangerous but the Forestry Commission is actively engaged in replanting and hopefully one day the Avenue will return to its former glory. Grand Avenue was originally planted in the mid-eighteenth century as the drive from the top of Forest Hill (on the A4) to Tottenham House which was until recently the residence of the Marquess of Ailesbury and is now a school. Half way along the Avenue, Eight Walks radiate in all directions across the Forest at the site of an old gibbet.

The Grand Avenue of Savernake Forest

The Green

It is appropriate to start a walk around the Town at the
Green since this is one of the Town's great beauty spots.
Historically the Green is of immence importance since it
is probably the site of the Anglo-Saxon settlement where
Marlborough began. Ownership of it was uncertain until
1893, when by mutual agreement it was decided that it
belonged to the Borough, and it is now preserved as one
of the Town's open spaces. Some of the cottage cellars on
the west and south side show evidence of very early
architecture. For centuries the Green was the centre of
community life and it is very easy to imagine the relaxed
atmosphere of medieval times without the main road
which now bisects it and often makes crossing a positive
hazard. But it is a tribute to the Town that, after so long,
the Green has been preserved as a place of beauty. The
avenue of limes is a pleasant feature well used to enhance
the atmosphere of many a photograph or painting.

The annual sheep fair was held on the Green until 1893
but a shift in emphasis in agriculture during this century
led to a decline in sheep numbers in the area, and it is
only with an increase more recently that the event has
been revived and is now held annually on the Common.

The Green – its south east corner

and from beneath its avenue of limes

A summer view of the Green with St. Mary's church behind

The west side – limes in autumn

The gabled house where William Golding lived

William Golding

Inside the porch of the gabled house to the north of the
churchyard path is a plaque recording the residents over
several centuries. Included is the local author William
Golding. His first ever piece of writing was called *The
Ladder and the Tree*. The tree, a lime, was in the back
garden of the house overlooking the churchyard and footpath. Jesse Chandler recalls playing with Golding as a boy
and climbing the tree to watch local residents pass by. It
was felled a few years ago.

St. Mary's Church
and
Patten Alley

St. Ellen's Cross was situated at the east side of the Green and was mentioned in a document of 1600. From here it is but a short walk along the tree-lined path to St. Mary's Church which overlooks the Green. It stands on the site of an early Saxon church which served the immediate community. It was damaged by the Great Fire of Marlborough in 1653 which started in the High Street and spread eastwards. There is mention of a church on this site in Domesday. In the twelfth century it was found inadequate and the present church was built in its place. It was restored during the Cromwellian era and it remains as an extremely fine example of Puritan architecture – one of the few in the country. From the tower of the church the whole of Marlborough can be seen and the photograph shows the view to the north west up Kingsbury Street with its fine houses.

This street can be reached from the church by walking along the passage between two shops known as Patten Alley. The Alley was so named because it was a quagmire and ladies going to church would wear pattens (thick irons strapped to their shoes) to cross the mud. The pattens were then removed before entering the church and hung on a shelf at the end of the Alley.

Views from St. Mary's Church tower — the Green

and Kingsbury Street

Patten Alley – 'a quagmire'

Kingsbury Street

Kingsbury Street divides the two parishes of St. Peter and St. Mary. This area was the old Kingsbury ward and the name suggests that it had some association with Royal property. Today it is the 'Fleet Street' of Marlborough, housing the offices of the two local newspapers, *The Marlborough Times* and *The Wiltshire Gazette and Herald*.

The second view of Kingsbury Street is taken from the site of the old town gallows some way up the hill. The gallows are recorded as being here in the twelfth century and executions were taking place certainly until the end of the Civil War. Two Welshmen were the last to be executed, in 1642. They were deserters from the Royalist forces. In 1627 James Hammond and his wife, Christopher Edmunds and his wife and Agnes Chilcot were hanged here. Their crime was burglary.

Kingsbury Street from the site of the old gibbet

On the opposite side of the road is Kingsbury Hill House School. At the top of the street was a bowling green and also the site of the Town Pound where straying cattle were impounded. It was later moved to just opposite the Convalescent Hospital, but was destroyed a few years ago.

The Common

A walk up the hill brings us to the Common with its expansive views across the Downs. The Common was originally part of the Norman Kings' Royal property which consisted of the Common – until recently known as 'The Thorns' – Savernake Forest and the Barton which included the Castle. It was eventually acquired by the Borough of Marlborough with an exchange of land in the reign of King John. It then became the Burgesses' common land on which they had a right to graze their cattle. Burgesses were certain elected owners of property who had paid property tax. Gradually over the centuries the old selective system changed to our present system of ratepayers.

At the northern end of the Common, on part of the eighteen hole golf course, is the Clump which has always been a local land mark. It is an iron age burial mound. The pine trees were planted on it in 1880 and, at the time of writing, are due for removal.

The Common is still used for a variety of local events. A regular event of the past was the Marlborough horse races which were held there until the end of last century.

The Clump on the Common – a local landmark

Clements Meadow, once home of Sir Gordon Richards

Clements Meadow

A turn out of Free's Avenue past the Convalescent
Hospital (originally the workhouse) brings us into an area
at the north west of the Town which contains a number
of large late-Victorian and Edwardian properties. The
photograph shows a typical example of one of these,
Clements Meadow, which was a previous residence of Sir
Gordon Richards, the famous race horse jockey and
trainer.

Walking down towards the Town centre from this
north-eastern end probably follows the angle of attack
used by the Royalist cavalry when they entered the Town
during the Civil War in December 1642.

The entrance to Horsepassage Yard next to the White Horse Bookshop

The Civil War

There is some controversy over which passage the Royalist
Cavalry forced to make their entry. Tradition has it that
they came in by Chandlers Yard which adjoins the White
Horse Bookshop. It was also known as Horsepassage Yard,
perhaps supporting the tradition. The present name
derives from Chandler the saddler who had his shop next
to the yard from 1803 to 1924. The rear of the building is a
fine example of pre Great Fire property. Very few buildings escaped the fire of 1653 and the rear of this is one of
the best examples of that time. In the attic is a beam which
carries the date 1559.

Horsepassage Yard – the Royalists came this way?

The Town Hall at the head of the High Street

The Town Hall

From this point the High Street and its imposing Town Hall can be well viewed. The High Cross originally stood at this end and so it has always been a focal point of the town. The first Town Hall replaced the High Cross in 1630 combining the function of Guildhall and Market Hall. It was destroyed by the Great Fire in 1653 at which time it housed the Borough records. A man named William Swindon risked his life by entering the burning building and dragging out the Town chest, so saving all the documents which give us so much of today's knowledge of the past. The grateful Corporation rewarded him with half-a-crown. The present Town Council still possesses the original chest.

Perrin's Hill

The Town Hall was rebuilt in 1654, again in 1793 and again in 1867. The present hall was built in 1902. Behind it is a stepped pathway, leading from the Parade to Kingsbury Street, named Perrin's Hill; it was previously called The Shoot.

There used to be a row of semi-permanent structures down the middle of the High Street from the Town Hall to about where the Castle & Ball stands, roughly the area now occupied by the Wednesday and Saturday markets. The buildings were mostly butchers' shops and were known as The Shambles. They too were destroyed by the fire of 1653 but were rebuilt. They were finally demolished in 1812.

Perrin's Hill which used to be known as The Shoot

Alma Place – the best example of a true stable yard

Alma Place

On the south side of the High Street, between numbers 11 and 12, is the entrance to a yard known as Alma Place. It contains twelve dwellings which originally served The Angel, an important stage-coach inn, which stood on the site of the present Southern Electricity showrooms. The cottages were formally stabling and accommodation for ostlers. The name suggests that it was converted to cottages at about the time of the Crimean War. There are several yards on the south side of the High Street some of which also contained stables. Others were thoroughfares to the slaughterhouses, private houses and the Mill. Alma Place is the best example of a true stable yard which was *not* used as a thoroughfare.

The Priory from its gardens

The Priory

About half way along the High Street on the lower side is the entrance to the Priory and its gardens. The original Priory was founded on this site by the White Friars or Carmelites in 1316. Although the present building only dates from about 1820 it was built using some of the material from the old building. Extensions were made to it in 1977 to accommodate an old people's home under the management of the Town Council.

The Priory Gardens which extend down to the river Kennet were given to the Borough as a gift by Mrs Tomasine Clay, in memory of her husband. There is a pleasant walk which extends along the south bank of the River.

The Gardens & The Kennet

Entrance to the Priory Gardens is by Figgins Lane. This lane has changed its name several times in the past. In 1316 it was named Dame Isbell's Lane. Dame Isbell was King Edward II's queen. It later became known as Lovell's Lane because John Lovell, five times Mayor of Marlborough, owned property nearby. In 1700 the name changed to Frigginswell Lane, after a local nearby landowner called 'Friggins' and because of the 'well' or spring in the adjacent Priory garden. In 1770 it was referred to as Isbury Lane, which was a continuation of the lane on the south side of the River. Today the old name of Frigginswell remains in a corrupted form, as Figgins Lane.

A short walk westwards along George Lane brings us to the Pewsey road bridge over the River Kennet. This bridge was built in 1924 replacing the earlier one of 1798. It was also known at one time as Ducks Bridge because James Duck owned a meadow just across the River, and as Cow Bridge after an inn called the Red Cow which was on Granham Hill. 'Kennet' is a Celtic name of unknown meaning but it is suggested that, as the Romans named their settlement at Mildenhall *Cunetio*, the nearby River Kennet may have been known as *Cunet*. The present name might easily have developed from this.

The Priory Gardens from the River walk

The River Kennet from the Pewsey road bridge

Treacle Bolley

The corner at the top of Granham Hill gives a delightful view of the Town. In the foreground of the photograph is the line of the old packhorse track which was the original trackway from Marlborough, via Treacle Bolley, up the hill and on to Pewsey. Treacle Bolley remains at the bottom of the hill as a footpath beside the River where the old Castle Mill stood. It is said that the name derives from the local miller addressing his barrel-shaped pony – 'Get up there old treacle belly'. This name was later transferred to the well known steamed puddings provided by Marlborough College mess hall, all of which became known as 'College Bolley'.

The College lies northwards from here, a public school which was opened in 1843. It is on the site of two important historical buildings.

The old packhorse road from Marlborough to Pewsey on Granham Hill

The Castle Mound

The Castle mound is the first historic site. It is tucked away among the buldings and its origin is unknown. It is certainly prehistoric, probably dating from the time of nearby Silbury Hill which also remains an enigma. The mound was eventually used to build the Castle keep after King William's acquisition, in the eleventh century. The first building, of about 1080, was wooden. Stone was first used in about 1175.

Henry I spent Easter here in 1110 and King Stephen beseiged the Castle in 1139 which was then held by a local baron, John Fitzgilbert. Beckett spent Christmas here with Henry II and in 1186 the King was at Marlborough Castle with the King of Scotland. King John was married in the Castle chapel to Avice, daughter of the Earl of Gloucester, in 1189. It was also used as his treasury. Perhaps the most important event which concerned the Castle was when Henry III held a parliament here in 1267 and the Statute of Marlborough was passed giving the common people some freedom from the barons. It was under seige several times during the Civil War.

The aerial view from above this end of the Town shows the Castle mound hidden in a clump of trees. The cover photograph also shows quite clearly the Town's two separate communities: the Saxon settlement of the north east end and the Norman settlement in the south-west or foreground of the picture. The High Street gradually linked the two.

Aerial view of the Town with the Castle mound covered by trees in the foreground

Marlborough College

Marlborough College itself includes the second famous building, 'C' House, which stands at the southern end of the Courtyard and is easily recognised by its pillared portico. The present house was built in 1702–15 as the mansion of the Duke of Somerset. It became the Castle Inn in 1751 and for nearly a hundred years it had the reputation of being the most famous coaching inn on the London–Bath Road. In its heyday, forty coaches changed horses here daily. The inn provided sixty beds, twelve post-carriages and more than sixty horses for its travellers, but with the coming of the railways the Castle Inn ceased to function.

The College itself began as a public school, primarily for the sons of clergymen, with about 200 boys. Since those early days it has expanded considerably and widened its horizons. Subsequently, new buildings were added and playing fields made. The chapel was built in 1886.

The Memorial Hall was opened in 1924 by the Duke of Connaught. Inside are recorded the names of 1,165 Old Marlburians who died in the First and Second World Wars. Decorations awarded them for gallantry are too numerous to mention; enough to say that thirteen Victoria Crosses and one George Cross have been awarded to Old Marlburians.

College Court with 'C' House – the old Castle Inn, right (above), left (below)

The College Memorial Hall

Preshute Church

West from here is the Town's third Anglican Church, known as Preshute. It was mentioned in Marlborough as early as 1091. In 1223, Preshute, St. Mary's and St. Peter's are all mentioned as being churches of Marlborough. Preshute was the oldest with a parish extending as far as Hackpen in the north and Elcot in the east, its southern boundary being the Forest. St. Mary's and St. Peter's parishes were later derived from that of Preshute.

Preshute Church – the oldest

St. Peter's Church

Moving back to the Town we enter the High Street, passing St. Peter's Church which was built in the mid-fifteenth century on the site of an earlier foundation. Sadly it was declared redundant in 1974, but the St. Peter's Church Trust was formed to preserve the building for the public and it is now used for various community and cultural purposes. It also contains the Town's Tourist Information Office. It remains as a fine example of Perpendicular church architecture. In March 1498 Thomas Wolsey, the son of an Ipswich butcher, who became Cardinal, Archbishop of York and Chanceller of the Kingdom, was ordained priest here in St. Peter's Church. The road which enters Marlborough from the west narrows, skirting the church, and has been the scene of many accidents. The possible removal of the church for a road-widening scheme was discussed several years ago but thankfully this idea was never taken seriously and so this fine church remains.

On the north side of the church stands a row of pleasant, small properties which escaped the Great Fire of 1653. The rear of some of these buildings shows evidence of fourteenth and fifteenth-century architecture. They remain as some of the oldest properties in Marlborough.

The Norman Church of St. Peter

Part of the High Street which escaped the Great Fire

The Sun Inn

Close by St. Peter's Church is the Sun Inn which, with its neighbours, also escaped the Great Fire. There is evidence of early architecture and the public bar contains some very fine interior panelling which is probably Elizabethan. It has been an inn since 1750.

St. Peter's Church from the Sun Inn

The High Street

Marlborough High Street is one of the widest streets in England, containing a great range of varying architecture. Its beauty is further enhanced by having an imposing church at each end. To the north-east is St. Mary's which was the centre of the Anglo-Saxon settlement and to the south-west is St. Peter's close to the Norman influence based on the Castle. The High Street gradually evolved, linking the two communities into one Marlborough. Most of the present buildings on the High Street were built after the Great Fire. Some of them date from 1654, though in many cases they have undergone some re-building. Examples are, The Castle & Ball, Duck's Toyshop, the Tudor Cafe and parts of others on the north side east of the Post Office. Since then, buildings date from various times, with each century adding its own sample of architecture including several from the present century which tend to excite local opinion.

There still remain in places sections of the pillared covered way which once extended along the length of the High Street on both sides. This is known locally as the Penthouse and was originally built to keep people dry when they went shopping. A large section remains along the north side, but south of the Town Hall little remains. It is now protected by law.

A more recent fire badly damaged one of the old 1654 rebuildings – the Polly Tearooms. The upstairs section was burned down and has not been replaced.

Marlborough High Street from St. Peter's Church tower

The Hermitage

Next to the Sun Inn is Hyde Lane. An older name for it was Blind Lane. Along this lane on the left is The Hermitage, on the site of a house which was dedicated for the use of a hermit in 1524 but was swept away at the Reformation. The land was conveyed to the Corporation for the maintenance of St. Peter's Church. John Lawrence built a house on this site in 1628 which was later extended to the west, the original outside wall now existing in the middle of the present house. It was in this house that the local Roman Catholics met secretly to celebrate Mass, for at that time it had been declared illegal. A Mr Hyde lived here in 1745 and it is from him that the lane is named. On the front wall can be seen a fire insurance plate of the kind which was fairly common from the eighteenth century onwards. In those days a householder, to protect himself from fire, would pay an insurance fee to an insurance company in return for which a plaque was placed on his wall. In the event of a fire the local fire tender and its men (usually employed by one or more of the insurance companies) would rush to the scene and attempt to extinguish the fire. Help could not be relied upon by householders not possessing a plaque.

The Hermitage and its fire insurance plaque

The High Street – site of the Great Fire

The Great Fire

Returning now to the High Street, it was on the lower side in the vicinity of the Ivy House Hotel that the Great Fire of Marlborough began. It started at the premises of a leather tanner and it was the bark of dried oak, which was used in the tanning process, which kindled the fire. A south-westerly wind swept the fire eastwards and the southern side of the High Street was almost destroyed, though the Priory, which stood back from the road, escaped. The flames were carried to the north side and nearly all the properties east of the site of the Post Office were destroyed. The Town Hall was lost and St. Mary's Church suffered severe damage.

The south side of the High Street along which the Fire swept

Two Yards

A group of shops between numbers 106 and 107 High Street is called Hughenden Yard. It is known locally as the Arcade and was recently opened up and improved, it gets its name from the local Free family, who owned it and adjacent property, because some generations ago the family moved to Marlborough from Hughenden in Buckinghamshire.

Between numbers 120 and 121 High Street is Neates Yard which was named after two brothers Neate, carpenters and undertakers, who had their workshops here in the late nineteenth century. An earlier name for it was Coombes Yard, after a Coombes who was in business here and also a carpenter and undertaker.

Hughenden Yard . . .

. . . and Neates Yard – a quiet backwater

Russell Square – the gable end of the old White Hart Inn

White Hart Inn

The entrance to Russell Square is between numbers 115 and 116 High Street. This is one of the Town's more famous places. The picture shows the gable end of the old White Hart Inn, 1453–1703. It was destroyed in the Great Fire and rebuilt in 1654. Samuel Pepys stayed here in 1668. A fine gallery around the rear of the old inn was demolished in 1970. The Square (the old inn yard) is also known as 'The Old Theatre' from the legend that Shakespeare sometimes played here with his travelling company of players after 1602 when the use of the Guildhall, a few doors away, was forbidden them, due to previous damage and fear of the plague. The present name comes from F.M. Russell who traded here in 1832.

The Old Rope Factory

A right turn past the Bear Hotel near the Town Hall leads into the Parade which because of its lower position near the River was previously known as The Marsh. The photograph shows one of the oldest buildings in the Town, the Old Rope Factory. It escaped the Great Fire of 1653 despite the fact that, like most of the buildings in the Town, its roof was of thatch. By an act of 1654, all roofs were to be of tile, slate or stone. Incidentally the devastation to the Town was such that Oliver Cromwell declared Marlborough to be a national disaster area. For the 250 years until 1960 this building was a rope factory. Recently it has been referred to as Katharine House.

The Old Rope Factory

St. Peter's & St. John's

Nearby, at the corner of the Parade, is St. Peter's School which now accommodates children of junior school age. It stands on the site of the Hospital of St. John, a mixed religious community founded before 1215. From 1550 until 1962 it was the Grammar School which then moved to new buildings on the hill south of the Town. During the reorganisation of secondary education it became the Comprehensive School of St. John's, together with the Secondary Modern School then housed in new premises below the Forest at Chopping Knife Lane.

The present junior school building dates from 1905. The lawn between the school and the Old Rope Factory was the site of an Elizabethan workhouse until a new Union workhouse was built adjoining the Common in 1836.

St. Peter's School on an ancient site

St. John's School on the hill

Marlborough looking back from the Bath Road

Who? What? Where? and When?

Alan Sutton

Answers in

MARLBOROUGH
in old photographs